Doodle Devotional

VOLUME 1

PSALM 23

Psalm 23

by
Keren A. Threlfall

with
Daniel Threlfall

Doodle Devotional

VOLUME 1

PSALM 23

Flourish Media
a division of Awesomesauce Publishing

Visit http://awesomesaucepublishing.com/psalm23 for updates and giveaways!

Fonts used in art: Bonjour, Fox and Bear, Faith and Glory, Handsome Hand, Hunterswood, and Have Heart One. (Used with commercial license.)

First edition: December 2015

Printed in the United States of America

Psalm 23

Welcome to the Psalm 23 Doodle Devotional!

This is a devotional book intended for you to doodle in, color, and maybe even tear out a few pages!

Our Doodle Devotional will walk you through the text of Psalm 23 with our devotional material, also creating space for you to doodle and color the text.

By designing this book as we did, our goal is to help you meditate on and deepen your familiarity with Psalm 23. Our desire is that you will come away treasuring this passage as though it is a dear, familiar friend.

Psalm 23 is only six verses long, also making it an easy passage to commit to memory. As you linger over the text, you will not only create beautiful artwork, but the words of Psalm 23 will be stored in your mind and heart for years to come.

Note: Because of the classic familiarity of this particular passage, we have chosen to use the
King James Version in these doodles, but we encourage you to study this text in the translation that is most familiar to you. Our devotional material will also include portions of the passage using other translations.

What is a devotional, anyway?

A devotional is simply a tool to help you study the Bible. Usually, it breaks down passages or topics from the Bible in a way that is easier to digest. Devotionals can make studying the Bible more appealing and accessible. A good devotional is designed to help you *devote* yourself to grow in your relationship with God; but you certainly don't need one to study the Bible on your own.

How and Why to Study the Bible

In the New Testament, Jesus tells us that the greatest commandment is to "love the Lord your God with all your heart and with all your soul and with all your mind." Part of loving God is loving Him with our *minds*, and this includes the study of the Bible.

To better understand any smaller passage of Scripture, it is crucial that we study its context and placement within the whole of Scripture and within chronological and cultural contexts. It is also important that we not reduce Bible study to a collection of truisms or cherry-picked verses to meet our need of the hour. It is true that even small portions of God's Word are powerful, and that God's Spirit often uses His Word to comfort us, encourage us, rebuke us, and remind us. But it is unwise to take only small portions at a time without understanding the context as a whole.

In her book, *Women of the Word*, Jen Wilkin encourages her readers to use three questions as a framework for examining each passage:

- What does it say?
- What does it mean?
- How should it change me?

By consistently evaluating each passage we encounter using these questions as a framework, we will grow to better love and understand God's Word.

As you look at Psalm 23, we encourage you to evaluate this passage with these questions in mind. (Feel free to doodle them in!)

While this devotional will guide you through this process, this framework will set you up to be able to learn from any passage of the Bible, even when there is no accompanying devotional.

In the back of this book, we have included an appendix that features resources for understanding Bible study and some resources specific to Psalm 23.

An Overview of Psalm 23

Psalm 23 is one of the most loved, most quoted, and best recognized passages of Scripture.

But do we truly know what it means and how God intended us to understand it?

By examining Psalm 23 as whole within its context, then carefully studying each phrase, we can gain a clearer understanding of this passage's meaning.

The book of Psalms is part of the Old Testament. The title of the book in Hebrew means "songs of praises." Each psalm was written as poetry, but this book is more than a collection of poems; the book of Psalms is a collection of *songs*. These songs can be classified into five different types: hymns, communal laments, royal songs, personal laments, and songs of personal thanksgiving.

In the Old Testament, the name used for God is frequently written as YHWH, or *Yahweh*. It is this name by which God revealed Himself to Moses on Mount Sinai, as *I Am*. And this is the name by which God is referred to in Psalm 23.

Focusing on Psalm 23

Hermann Gunkel, the theologian who classified the psalms into five divisions, gave to Psalm 23 a classification that may surprise some: Psalm 23 is a psalm of lament.

Although it is a lament, *a song of longing*, we also see the psalmist's confident trust in Yahweh. As the psalm progresses, the author moves toward assurance, confidence, and trust. It is as if the author says, "This is not the end. Look what God is going to do because He is the Good Shepherd! I rest in Him. He takes my complaint and turns it into comfort."

And there is likely no other book of Scripture to which believers have turned to for comfort and assurance more readily than the book of Psalms.

This psalm, or hymn, is divided into two main parts: the first four verses focus on Yahweh as Shepherd, and the final two verses depict the Lord as host of the feast.

David knew what it was to be both shepherd and king, but most of his readers would have been more familiar with shepherds than with kings.

While some view the depiction of the Lord as Shepherd as a paradoxical combination of highest exaltation with utter lowliness, others believe that "Lord as Shepherd" was not necessarily paradoxical, but more of an articulate portrayal of the complexity of the nature of God.

Regardless, it is clear that as Shepherd, He is one who cares for, tends to, and guides His flock, His people.

Psalm 23

1

The Lord is my shepherd; I shall not want.

2

He maketh me to lie down in green pastures: He leadeth me beside the still waters.

3

He restoreth my soul: He leadeth me in the paths of righteousness for His name's sake.

4

Yea, though I walk through the valley of the shadow of death, I will fear no evil: for Thou art with me; Thy rod and Thy staff they comfort me.

5

Thou preparest a table before me in the presence of mine enemies: Thou anointest my head with oil; my cup runneth over.

6

Surely goodness and mercy shall follow me all the days of my life: and I will dwell in the house of the Lord for ever.

Psalm 23

Verse 1

The Lord is my shepherd; I shall not want. (KJV)

The Lord is my shepherd, I lack nothing. (ESV)

The Lord is my shepherd.

This image of Lord as Shepherd is woven throughout both Old and New Testament Scripture. But in this particular passage, the relationship of the shepherd to the lamb is that of a tender, individual caretaker. He is *my* shepherd.

David was a shepherd-king, foreshadowing Christ himself; and like Christ, he filled both the roles of humble shepherd and eventual triumphant king. For David, being a shepherd was not just a metaphor, but the reality of his pre-king years.

To us, the shepherd is a foreign and unfamiliar career choice. It is an occupation cloaked in idyllic unknowns and romanticized by paintings of beautiful fields of green. But for the people who lived in David's time the shepherd was a common laborer, an occupation nearly everyone was familiar with.

Of this, theologian Derek Kidner wrote, "David uses the most comprehensive and intimate metaphor yet encountered in the Psalms, preferring usually the more distant 'king' or 'deliverer', or the impersonal 'rock', 'shield', etc.; whereas the shepherd lives with his flock and is everything to it: guide, physician and protector." (*Psalms 1-72*, Downers Grove: InterVarsity Press, 1973, pp. 109-110.)

I shall not want.

Our Shepherd is our provider. David proclaimed that even in the midst of difficult seasons, he would not lack what he needed. The words of the English Standard Version are simple, yet awe-inducing: "I lack nothing."

The Shepherd is a capable caretaker and provider. All my true needs are satisfied through Him. At times, many distractions draw us away from this truth. Sometimes we need a gentle reminder; sometimes we need to taste His goodness again to remember.

It is remarkable how well these words from Audrey Assad's song, *"I Shall Not Want,"* capture this theme:

> From the love of my own comfort
> From the fear of having nothing
> From a life of worldly passions
> Deliver me, O God
>
> From the need to be understood
> From the need to be accepted
> From the fear of being lonely
> Deliver me, O God
> Deliver me, O God
>
> And I shall not want, I shall not want
> When I taste Your goodness I shall not want
> When I taste Your goodness I shall not want

We can also remember to look at this portion from the perspective of God being both Shepherd and King. He is Yahweh, and He is a caring shepherd. This is a comfort to those who are His flock.

Food for Thought

1. How can you see the Lord as guide, physician, and protector in your life?

2. What are evidences of God's personal shepherding and leading in your life?

3. What are areas are you sometimes forgetful of God's provision?

The Lord
is my Shepherd;
I shall
not want.

Psalm 23:1

The Lord is my shepherd; I shall not want.

He maketh me to lie down in green pastures: He leadeth me beside the still waters.

He restoreth my soul: He leadeth me in the paths of righteousness for His name's sake.

Yea, though I walk through the valley of the shadow of death, I will fear no evil: for Thou art with me; Thy rod and Thy staff they comfort me.

Thou preparest a table before me in the presence of mine enemies: Thou anointest my head with oil; my cup runneth over.

Surely goodness and mercy shall follow me all the days of my life: and I will dwell in the house of the Lord for ever.

The Lord is my Shepherd; I shall not want.

Verse 2

He maketh me to lie down in green pastures: He leadeth me beside the still waters. (KJV)

He makes me lie down in green pastures, He leads me beside still waters, (ESV)

He maketh me to lie down in green pastures.

Here, the author of the psalm reflects on his experience as part of the Shepherd's flock. The leading here is indicative of gentle, gracious guiding.

He leads us not only to pastures, but makes us lie down in pastures that are rich and well-nourished.

In Phillip Keller's classic book on this text, *A Shepherd Looks at Psalm 23,* he notes that in order for sheep to lie down, there are four requirements:

- they must be free of fear
- they must not be fighting with each other
- they must be free of pests
- they must be free from hunger

God's flock needs to be in a state of peace to be able to come to this point. Jesus spoke of this peace when he said, "Peace I leave with you; my peace I give to you. Not as the world gives do I give to you. Let not your hearts be troubled, neither let them be afraid" (John 14:27).

God, as our Shepherd, is the only one who can lead us into a place of peace and rest.

He leadeth me beside the still waters.

The "green pastures" and "still waters" refer to the sheep's complete provision. She has protection. She has rest. She has food. She has water. She has all she needs.

Many of us have faced times of hardship — the days in which we run low on energy, patience, time, or emotional strength. God understands our needs.

As our shepherd, he not only sees our needs, but he meets our needs. He knows the frailty and helplessness of sheep. That is why he must *make* us to lie down. We often don't realize our own limits, but God in his graciousness makes us rest. He leads us to water.

food for thought

1. How is your Shepherd directing your life toward a place of rest?

2. How have you experienced green pastures or still waters?

3. What needs will you bring to your Shepherd in prayer?

HE MAKETH
ME TO LIE DOWN
IN GREEN PASTURES:
HE LEADETH ME BESIDE
THE STILL WATERS.

Psalm 23:2

The Lord is my shepherd; I shall not want.

He maketh me to lie down in green pastures: He leadeth me beside the still waters.

He restoreth my soul: He leadeth me in the paths of righteousness for His name's sake.

Yea, though I walk through the valley of the shadow of death, I will fear no evil: for Thou art with me; Thy rod and Thy staff they comfort me.

Thou preparest a table before me in the presence of mine enemies: Thou anointest my head with oil; my cup runneth over.

Surely goodness and mercy shall follow me all the days of my life: and I will dwell in the house of the Lord for ever.

HE MAKETH
ME TO LIE DOWN
IN GREEN PASTURES:
HE LEADETH ME BESIDE
THE STILL WATERS.

Psalm 23:3

Verse 3

He restoreth my soul: He leadeth me in the paths of righteousness for His name's sake. (KJV)

He restores my soul. He leads me in paths of righteousness for his name's sake. (ESV)

He restoreth my soul.

Take in the sound of that word — *restores*. It's a yearning word, something we all crave in our deepest soul. Restoration: for all to be made right, to be made as it ought to be.

In order to understand *how* to be restored, we need to know *what* it is to be restored. Notice how this phrase is surrounded by the same two phrases: "He leads me."

He leads me…He restores my soul…He leads me.

This "lead" on both sides of the verse is the key to unlocking this passage. He leads. We follow. Thereby, we are restored.

That is what we do — we follow our Good Shepherd, the One who completes us, fulfills us, rescues us, redeems us, feeds us, cares for us, and leads us.

As our leader, He will guide us towards following Him. We don't need to work longer, try harder, pray more fervently, or grit our teeth with more self-determination.

As we follow Him, here is how we experience soul restoration:

We walk in His community. A sheep alone is a sheep that is vulnerable, helpless, and likely to get lost. A sheep among her flock will be protected, corrected, and guided towards safety. Community is a balm to our soul.

We accept His protection. Notice how the psalm is interwoven with soul-restoring phrases. Some of these speak to our Shepherd's protection: "Fear no evil," "Your rod and your staff," "Presence of my enemies."

He is our defense. In order for our souls to thrive, we must be protected. The only adequate source of protection is our mighty Shepherd.

We cherish His comfort. God delights in giving us pleasure and abundance — the full table, the overflowing cup, the peace from strife. Our Shepherd gives these gifts to restore our souls.

Where does this leave us? It leaves us in a position of flourishing in His grace.

Restoration will come whether we are fighting it or seeking it, and maybe when we're least expecting it.

The Good Shepherd will restore your soul.

He leadeth me in the paths of righteousness for His name's sake.

Whatever our human conceptions of leadership are, we would do well to completely set them aside when we consider the leadership of our Good Shepherd.

Our Shepherd's leadership is like nothing else. It is a place of soul-restoring safety and peace. As we consider His perfect leading, let's look at the *where, why,* and *how* of this leading.

Where He leads us: paths of righteousness.

Our Shepherd leads us on paths. The Hebrew word for "path" refers to a path in a metaphorical sense, denoting a lifestyle choice (see Job 24:13; Psalm 119:105).

The focus, then, is not on the destination, but the journey. Regardless of where we're at on this path — miles ahead, lagging behind, stumbling along — we can be confident that we are on the right one.

Because He is leading us, we know that we are on a path of true blessing and fulfillment.

Why He leads us: for His name's sake.

In this passage, we aren't told the destination of the path, but we do know the purpose.

Why would God go to such pain and trouble to lead us? (See Hebrews 2:18 for more on that pain.) Because it is in keeping with His character.

That phrase "name's sake" is the concept of God acting in accord with His character.

What's the outcome of this? He is honored. God is glorified when His character is revealed in His leadership.

How He leads us: in a soul-restoring way.

Look at the phrase above — "He restores my soul." This is a soul-restoring, life-changing, heart-transforming, deeply fulfilling kind of leadership — leadership like you've never known, but always wanted.

God leads us in order to restore our souls, to fulfill His character, to place us on a path to righteousness, and to bring glory to His name.

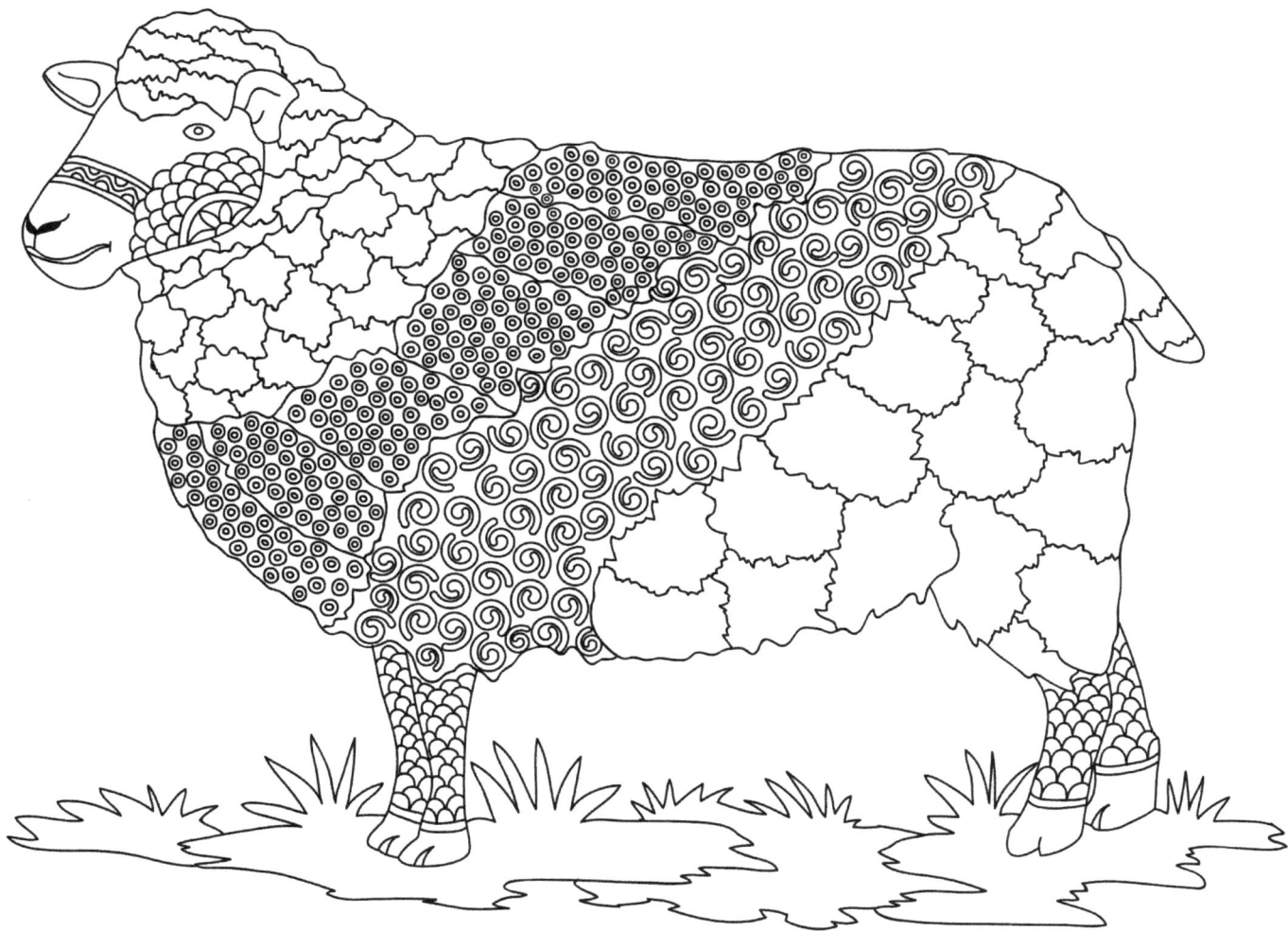

Food for Thought

1. Does your soul crave restoration?

2. What are some ways God has given restoration to your soul?

3. How has God shown you that His leading is the right path? (Consider the *where, why,* and *how* of His leading.)

he restoreth
my soul: he leadeth
me in the paths
of righteousness
for his
name's sake.

Psalm 23:3

The Lord is my shepherd; I shall not want.

He maketh me to lie down in green pastures: He leadeth me beside the still waters.

He restoreth my soul: He leadeth me in the paths of righteousness for His name's sake.

Yea, though I walk through the valley of the shadow of death, I will fear no evil: for Thou art with me; Thy rod and Thy staff they comfort me.

Thou preparest a table before me in the presence of mine enemies: Thou anointest my head with oil; my cup runneth over.

Surely goodness and mercy shall follow me all the days of my life: and I will dwell in the house of the Lord for ever.

he restoreth my soul: he leadeth me in the paths of righteousness for his name's sake.

Psalm 23:4

Verse 4

Yea, though I walk through the valley of the shadow of death, I will fear no evil: for thou art with me; thy rod and thy staff they comfort me. (KJV)

Even though I walk through the valley of the shadow of death, I will fear no evil, for you are with me; your rod and your staff they comfort me. (ESV)

Yea, though I walk through the valley of the shadow of death,

"The valley of the shadow of death" is a metaphor that we can all understand, because we have all faced such times. We have faced valleys of discouragement. We have feared for our lives. We've been wronged by others. We have walked through times of confusion, hurt, and misunderstanding.

These experiences are part of life even for a "righteous" person (Psalm 34:19).

I will fear no evil: for thou art with me; thy rod and thy staff they comfort me.

David understood difficulties. His life was characterized by war, political intrigue, family strife, and personal failings. He was hunted like an animal, exiled from the very nation he ruled, and ostracized by his family. David even sinned deeply, bringing shame upon himself, his family, and the nation Israel.

This is the valley of the shadow of death. And in the middle of these circumstances, David can be confident that his Good Shepherd will lead him through the difficult times.

The Rod

Shepherds used this simple stick for two purposes: to count their sheep and to protect them from dangerous wild animals. God knows each ones of us, just as a shepherd keeps track of each of his sheep. God protects us, as a shepherd would defend his sheep from predators.

The Staff

This is the familiar shepherd's crook — a long stick with a curved end. It is the shepherd's most important tool. He uses it gently to bring a lamb to its mother, to guide sheep into a different path, or to rescue sheep from a difficult place. The staff reminds us that God is gentle. He cares, protects, and nurtures us even through life's most difficult seasons.

When we feel as if life's circumstances cannot be any worse, we find hope in remembering God's loving care.

We feel the tender care of our Shepherd, counting us, carrying us, protecting us, and leading us onward to something glorious. In our lowest of lows when we feel pain beyond just the trial of the moment, we often feel utterly abandoned.

And yet, this glorious reality is given to us: God Himself is with us. His presence drives away all fear. God also ministers comfort to our hearts through His rod and staff, the tools of our always-present Shepherd.

food for thought

1. Recall one or two of the lowest points of your life.

2. Consider that God was with you in those moments. How does that bring comfort to your heart?

3. What ways have you allowed fear of evil to overcome the peace that God's presence brings?

Yea, though
I walk through the
valley of the shadow of
death, I will fear no evil:
for Thou art with me, Thy
rod and Thy staff they
comfort me.

Psalm 23:4

The Lord is my shepherd; I shall not want.

He maketh me to lie down in green pastures: He leadeth me beside the still waters.

He restoreth my soul: He leadeth me in the paths of righteousness for His name's sake.

Yea, though I walk through the valley of the shadow of death, I will fear no evil: for Thou art with me; Thy rod and Thy staff they comfort me.

Thou preparest a table before me in the presence of mine enemies: Thou anointest my head with oil; my cup runneth over.

Surely goodness and mercy shall follow me all the days of my life: and I will dwell in the house of the Lord for ever.

Yea, though I walk through the valley of the shadow of death, I will fear no evil: for Thou art with me; Thy rod and Thy staff they comfort me.

Psalm 23:5

Verse 5

Thou preparest a table before me in the presence of mine enemies: thou anointest my head with oil; my cup runneth over. (KJV)

You prepare a table before me in the presence of my enemies; you anoint my head with oil; my cup overflows. (ESV)

Thou preparest a table before me in the presence of mine enemies.

In verse five, the psalm takes a new direction. Instead of the imagery of sheep and shepherd, we are now watching a generous host spread a luxurious banquet.

In the previous verse, we read about life's lowest moments. Now, we read of life's greatest delights — prosperity, abundance, peace, and serenity.

Thou anointest my head with oil; my cup runneth over.

It would be easy to try to explain away each of the metaphors as referring to spiritual abundance and spiritual blessing, but that would miss the whole point of the passage. God delights in meeting both spiritual and physical needs.

The abundance that David writes about is just as real as the dangers he described. God prepares a table for us, showing that He provides for our physical needs. He anoints our heads with oil, showing that He shows honor to us. Our cup overflows, showing that there is no end to God's lavish gifts.

Each of these images — the table, the peace with enemies, the oil, and the overflowing cup — were part of lavish feasts in the ancient Near East. Prosperous men who conquered their foes would treat their guests to a full banquet, complete with anointing, the finest food, and bottomless drinks.

The progress of the psalm suggests that we may not experience this blessing until our final rest in eternity. Our trials will eventually come to an end. We will dwell in serenity with our Shepherd. Our enemies are banished. Our cup overflows in the eternity of abundance.

This is how God treats us. We are His honored guests and His cherished friends — for now and for eternity.

Food for Thought

1. How has God supplied for your spiritual needs in abundance?

2. How has God supplied your material needs?

3. What are you most looking forward to about eternity?

THOU PREPAREST
A TABLE BEFORE ME
IN THE PRESENCE OF
MINE ENEMIES: THOU
ANOINTEST MY HEAD WITH OIL;
MY CUP RUNNETH OVER.

Psalm 23:5

The Lord is my shepherd; I shall not want.

He maketh me to lie down in green pastures: He leadeth me beside the still waters.

He restoreth my soul: He leadeth me in the paths of righteousness for His name's sake.

Yea, though I walk through the valley of the shadow of death, I will fear no evil: for Thou art with me; Thy rod and Thy staff they comfort me.

Thou preparest a table before me in the presence of mine enemies: Thou anointest my head with oil; my cup runneth over.

Surely goodness and mercy shall follow me all the days of my life: and I will dwell in the house of the Lord for ever.

THOU PREPAREST
A TABLE BEFORE ME
IN THE PRESENCE OF
MINE ENEMIES: THOU
ANOINTEST MY HEAD WITH OIL;
MY CUP RUNNETH OVER.

Psalm 23:6

Verse 6

Surely goodness and mercy shall follow me all the days of my life: and I will dwell in the house of the Lord for ever. (KJV)

Surely goodness and mercy shall follow me all the days of my life, and I shall dwell in the house of the Lord forever. (ESV)

Surely goodness and mercy shall follow me all the days of my life:

The final verse of the psalm is its glorious climax. You can almost hear David shouting this stanza in a tone of triumph and victory.

There are two main themes in this verse: *forever* and *grace*.

The two words "goodness" and "mercy" are brimming with meaning. The word "good" refers to agreeable pleasure. "Mercy" is the Hebrew word *chesed*, which is God's unstoppable covenant love.

Taken together, the two words paint a picture of grace — God's favor that we don't deserve, can't repay, and hardly understand because it's so overwhelming.

And I shall dwell in the house of the Lord forever.

When David writes, "I shall dwell in the house of the Lord forever," he is expressing the reality of life with God. In ancient Hebrew thinking, God was seen as living in the temple or "house of the Lord" (Psalm 18:6). Thus, to dwell with God is to live in a state of constant worship (Psalm 27:4).

The psalm climaxes in the person of God himself. God is goodness. He is mercy. He is grace. He showed us this eternal grace when Jesus gave His life on the cross.

Psalm 23 opened with the statement, "The Lord is my shepherd." In the final verse, we experience its liberating truth — God's grace endures forever, bountifully bestowed on us in the person of Jesus Christ.

The Good Shepherd is also the Sacrificial Lamb (John 1:29). He is our eternal savior. And we can live in the glory of His unstoppable grace.

food for thought

1. How can you worship God in your daily life?

2. How have you experienced God's grace today?

3. How will God's constant presence impact your life?

Surely
goodness and mercy
shall follow me all the
days of my life: and I will
dwell in the house
of the Lord for
ever.

Psalm 23:6

The Lord is my shepherd; I shall not want.

He maketh me to lie down in green pastures: He leadeth me beside the still waters.

He restoreth my soul: He leadeth me in the paths of righteousness for His name's sake.

Yea, though I walk through the valley of the shadow of death, I will fear no evil: for Thou art with me; Thy rod and Thy staff they comfort me.

Thou preparest a table before me in the presence of mine enemies: Thou anointest my head with oil; my cup runneth over.

Surely goodness and mercy shall follow me all the days of my life: and I will dwell in the house of the Lord for ever.

Surely goodness and mercy shall follow me all the days of my life: and I will dwell in the house of the Lord for ever.

Reflecting on Psalm 23

Reflecting

So, it is in this manner that we focus in on the individual parts of the Psalm, seeing the big picture:

The Lord, Yahweh, is a shepherd who is personal, leading the individuals of His flock.

As the trustworthy, capable Shepherd, He gently leads His sheep.

He provides for His sheep so that they lack nothing they need.

He leads toward rest and good things.

We will all walk through very difficult times in life; but even in the darkest points of life, He is there with us, comforting us as our Shepherd.

The Good Shepherd is also the Great Host of the banquet.

We are the honored guests, and His feast is abundant.

May our hearts flourish in the truths God gives us in this passage.

Looking back, we can be reminded to ask ourselves again, these questions about the passage:

- What does it say?
- What does it mean?
- How should it change me?

Psalm 23

Appendix A
Resources for Studying Scripture

Women of the Word: How to Study the Bible with Both Our Hearts and Our Minds (Jen Wilkin)

His Word in My Heart: Memorizing Scripture for a Closer Walk With God (Janet Pope)

Appendix B
Resources to Accompany a Study of Psalm 23

Books

A Shepherd Looks at Psalm 23 (W. Phillip Keller)
Derek Kidner - Psalms 1-72, Psalms 73-150 (Tyndale Old Testament Commentary)

Music

"I Shall Not Want," from the album, *Fortunate Fall*, Audrey Assad
Psalm 23 for Kids, Patricia King & Steve Swanson
Psalms, Sandra McCracken (not specifically Psalm 23)
"Psalm 23 (Surely Goodness, Surely Mercy)," from the album, *Psalms, Vol. 2* Shane & Shane

Psalm 23

Thank you for working through The Psalm 23 Doodle Devotional.

See if you can write out Psalm 23 from memory:

Doodle Devotional

VOLUME 1

PSALM 23

To learn more about future Doodle Devotionals and other great books from

Awesomesauce Publishing, please visit

http://awesomesaucepublishing.com.

www.ingramcontent.com/pod-product-compliance
Lightning Source LLC
Chambersburg PA
CBHW0s1228040426

42445CB00016B/1913